# THE PYRAMIDS OF MALPIGHI

# THE PYRAMIDS OF MALPIGHI

STEVEN GEHRKE

*2002 Philip Levine Prize for Poetry*

*Selected by Philip Levine*

*Anhinga Press, 2004*
*Tallahassee, Florida*

Cover design, book design and production – C.L. Knight
Author photograph – Nadine Meyer
Cover art – *Intent 2,* digital painting by C.L. Knight

Typesetting – Titles set in Journal, text set in ITC New Century Light

Library of Congress Cataloging-in-Publication Data
*The Pyramids of Malpighi* by Steven Gehrke – First Edition
ISBN 0938078-76-3
Library of Congress Card Number: 2003106042

*This publication is sponsored in part by a grant from the Florida Department of State, Division of Cultural Affairs, and the Florida Arts Council.*

Anhinga Press Inc. is a nonprofit corporation dedicated wholly to the publication and appreciation of fine poetry.

For personal orders, catalogs
and information write to:
Anhinga Press
P.O. Box 10595
Tallahassee, FL 32302
Web site: www.anhinga.org
E-mail: info@anhinga.org

Published in the United States
by Anhinga Press
Tallahassee, Florida
First Edition, 2004

*for my parents*

CONTENTS

# ACKNOWLEDGMENTS

Grateful acknowledgments to the following journals:

*Flyway*: "At the Chinese Buffet"
*Georgia Review*: "The Invention of Pointillism" and "The Pyramids of Malpighi"
*Gulf Coast:* "Capitalism"
*Indiana Review*: "Manhole Covers and Lakes"
*Laurel Review*: "Secretarial School Graduation Dance, 1968"
*Many Mountains Moving*: "Adolescence"
*Meridian*: "Inside the Dialysis Machine"
*Notre Dame Review*: "Minnesota Landscape with a Painting In It"
*Rattle:* "Shingles"
*RUNES*: "1913"
*Tampa Review*: "In Celebration of My Father's 35$^{th}$ Year at the Coca-Cola Company" and "First Snow: A Memory"

"The Invention of Pointillism" received a Special Mention in the *2004 Pushcart Prize Anthology*; "Capitalism" won the *Gulf Coast Poetry Contest*

Sincere thanks to the following readers, who helped this manuscript grow into its current form: Philip Pardi, Darin Ciccotelli, Vive Griffith, Bruce Snider, Robert Lee, Eric Gravning, Susanna Childress, Jessica Garratt, Donald Mattingly, David Wevill, Thomas Whitbread, Sherod Santos, Lynne McMahon, Edward Micus, and most especially Nadine Meyer, for her love and support.

# THE PYRAMIDS OF MALPIGHI

*You cannot come to unity and remain material.*

— A.R. Ammons

# THE INVENTION OF POINTILLISM

## THE INVENTION OF POINTILLISM

Once, in the apartment of a woman I barely knew,
in a room made of blurred light and ashes
with carpet the color of very old newspaper,
I began to believe love was a collection of sighs
and small gestures that flew off as we moved.

I was foolish and romantic. I didn't know
that the sound of her children, splashing in the pool
outside her bedroom window, that the tips
of her husband's shoes aimed at me
from the closet, that even the print of Seurat's

*The Circus*, hung at an angle near the bed
would never leave me. Afterward, I stood
in her bathroom, watching a face (barely my own),
waver in my hand's cupped water,
not knowing that each cell remembers desire

the way each shard of the bottle shattered on the asphalt
outside her apartment remembered thirst,
the way the bones of the finch that lay next to the bottle,
equally shattered, remembered flight. I believed,
at climax, that each cell was thinking

one thought, or not thinking at all, but opening
like a tiny mouth to release its fraction of the soul.
I didn't know this meant I could never leave that
room. Do you see? Even now, I am that woman,
drawn and re-drawn in the light below the window,

I am the water crashing over the edge of the pool,
the darkness gathering in the bottom of the shoes,
in the spaces between the threads of the carpet.

I can even be the children, doing as they are told,
        choreographing, for the sake of the father,

their lies, like flashlights aimed at the night sky
        to re-create the moon. Do you see? I can be anything
in that room. Except, perhaps, for the husband.
        But if, some mornings, he sits with the paper,
pretending to read, but really watching his family orbit

        through the V of light as he turns the pages, as he believes,
stubbornly, in their goodness, what could
        be wrong with that? And if he wakes
some nights, driven from that place where he sleeps
        with only a small road of bed between him and his wife,

if he stands, suddenly, to adjust the picture on the wall,
        if he places one foot then the other onto carpet
the color of news that doesn't matter anymore, and stares
        into the face of each painted dot, which at this hour of night
would be clotted with darkness, and if he thinks

        not of the ballerina's foot slipping from the side of the horse,
the body of the tumbler bent grotesquely and disjointed,
        if instead he thinks, briefly and not for the first time,
*the only truth is the truth within a single cell*, even I will
        be forced to believe him. Do you see? We have

only two choices. We can believe, stubbornly, that the picture
        on the wall is whole. Or we can imagine
Seurat, as a boy, holding a fresh brush in his hand,
        thinking, "I will show them how easily
they are tricked," then narrowing the tip with his mouth.

## CAPITALISM

(THE MGM GRAND HOTEL AND CASINO, LAS VEGAS, NEVADA: 5 A.M.)

This is how the city has always worked
for you: you and a buddy, separated
for hours, arrive back at the room, simultaneously,
each of you hoping the other has won, each
hoping the other has something you can borrow.

Which is why, broke, you are on your way back down,
not knowing what you want, but letting the elevator
lock you in, as if inside a gaze, your reflection torn,
at random floors, by the metal on the door,
the way an image is torn by the eyes, then repaired.

It is late, yes, you are tired, but hunger has no stopping
point: it's a pocket with a hole that you fill and fill.
And in your delirium and thirst, the casino floor is a place
where gamblers spend all night digesting themselves,
the losers dumped out onto the street, the others sucked

into elevators and stairwells, like nutrients into a bloodstream.
It's all about scale: the fed cells, the lights flicking on
inside the rooms, the fantasy of slot machines — the velocity
of the dropped coin continued — that transfer
of inertia — undivided in its winnings. Yesterday, on television,

you learned how cloning works, the ovum emptied out,
like a purse onto a table, like an O, and, with a cell
from a fingertip — these are the words they used —
"an investment is made." The point, you suppose,
is that our bodies are lost and given back to us in change.

And now, as you walk and walk, past countless black jack dealers,
each gripped by half a table around the waist, you can't stop

clutching and releasing the last dumb coin in your pocket, you can't stop
entering your own vision, being pulled forward by it,
the mind extending its oars and drawing the seen world

back into itself. Which, at this moment, consists
of a jungle compressed into a few trees,
a pond, and two lions — yes, *Live Lions!*, it's there,
written on a plaque — who spend all night socketed
in their caves. You stand before the glass, wondering

if the casino noises are echoed back to them in sleep:
as the stuttering of slot machines? Hyena
and zebra screams? The elevators rise and fall behind you.
Passengers get off: they are swept back
into their bodies. The lions emerge from their caves,

shaking their muscles awake, their huge padded feet
noiseless on the stone. They are real, yes,
but watching them strip the overhead lights
from the surface of the pond, that violence
and beauty in their tongues, makes you believe

they've been sent by God, not as symbols,
but to dismantle the city, bit by bit, and bury it
in the desert, that it's possible, even in pieces,
for the city to stay lit, its presence measured by the tint
of neon to the sand. Desire is that permanent,

etched around the edges of the body, like the ring of light
at an eclipse, as if the body had stepped in front of it.
And you too, making fists inside your pocket and watching
the lions shake water from their faces, are part
of the illusion, part of a world they are shown

but cannot eat. This hungry, this broke, you understand
		that if one of them sniffs forward, the male you think,
and licks the glass, a transaction has been made —
		something lost, something won —
and that capitalism is the taste of Windex on his tongue.

## MINNESOTA LANDSCAPE WITH A PAINTING IN IT

— After Egon Schiele's *Etreinte (Les Amants)*

Skin smeared away, motion rising to the surface,
all the pores opening into screams,
you know the kind of painting I mean,
lovers sifting together, each a fish
caught in the widening stream of the other,
as if the artist believed form itself
to be a violence, our skin cast upon us
as a punishment for sin, for the lust
that tries, again and again, to work it away.

It's almost a law: what, at first,
seems romantic, turns ominous, so a second
glance reveals two fingers entering
his face where a cheek has washed away,
the blanket they lie upon unraveling
from between her legs, the wind, along the edges,
rubbing her hair into flames.

Outside, it is fall, and a little color smudges
the edges of things, like lipstick
smeared across the rim of a glass,
though it seems a little fake, the un-
shucked corn along the highway, each ear
"sleeved" in green, a leaf filling
with passion, "like a hand entering a dress,"

each image rushing towards metaphor,
flaring up to the edge of itself before it cools,
as the lovers cool on the blanket,
letting form take them again, oblivious
to the motion of the pillows beneath,
the ruffled borders breaking into teeth.

## AT THE CHINESE BUFFET

Not for any reason, but not just —
I am listening to four young
waitresses speaking in Chinese.
They sit in a booth
around a tray of wantons
and fold the wantons together
around lumps of cream cheese,
molding them into flowers
that others, days from now, will eat.
From this distance, they could be tucking
the stars into anesthetized sleep, hiding
snowflakes in tiny knapsacks.
From this distance, one might be saying,
*when I die, donate my hair*
*to the balding crows.*
Another, holding out her fingers,
*look, my bones would make*
*a lovely set of piano keys.*
Most likely, though, they speak
of simple things: the boss's new car,
what they've seen on TV,
how after work one of them
will soak her feet in salt water.
(But is the pan blue? Is the water
drawn through pipes that descend
from the wells of heaven?)
Is there anything lovely enough
to destroy the imagination?
Now the older girl teaches
the youngest to shape the wantons,
her fingers mending the dough-petals —
in English now — *pinch, pinch.*

## 1913

*(After Ernst Kirchner's* Berlin Street Scene*)*

something was about to be accomplished:
  a boot-heel poised above
the shovel's edge, smoke from a genie-bottle
  glimpsed, the renunciation
of an adage (this is history as summation,
  gavel-tapping proclamations) a kink
knocked loose from the ancestral chain:

Berlin: 1913: and Kirchner's at his window,
  looking playfully down the sight-line
of a brush, preparing to paint
  the error in: bolt in the cartwheel
loosening, a wind-tipped spittoon,
  the pickpocket drumming
his fingers on the railing: this is randomness

(what Kirchner calls the eenie-miney-moe
  of the mind) refigured, almost
perfectly, into moderness: the world made up in uni-
  form: the green-helmeted boys turtle
through the grass, and later, the colonel,
  in love with novelty, confirms the dead
by tapping each body with a piñata stick:

**

for three days — brushes forgotten in a dish
  of solvent, deflated hot air balloons
upon his pallet — he'd been refusing
  to paint: all color, he'd decided,
was a form of restraint: wax-drippings

on an envelope, innuendo meant
to flush the cheek, meant to suffocate a face,

or himself, thirteen years ago, painting
a severed wing in pinks and greens
and nailing it to his mother's door: this,
is the day of the invention of the X-ray,
of news, from the United States, of a doctor
who, using the machine, lowered clamp
into a chest and, though the body had learned

to cling to it, pulled a nail from the darkness
of a young boy's lung: how romantic,
Kirchner thinks, to paint like that, to do away
with the exterior and look straight down
into the pain: this woman, for instance, walking
home, straight-lined, lips like a diary-lock,
a scarf trailing down her back like a horse's mane,

if she carries in her purse, a choral-
soaked rag for lifting to the nose,
a way to forget more precisely, to trim
back the bramble of the mind, if she thinks
of her own history as asphyxiation,
even if he could lift the fingerprint
of consciousness from her gravid face,

soak her onto the tip of his brush and hoist
her from the street, could he make audible
even one note of her *shivered prayer*, the secret anthem
playing in her brain: no: all he can do
is add his deception to the scene:

a bricklayer trying to wall
the horizon in, history smothered beneath

the ticker-tape of collective imagery:
airplane photos, chalk-board strategy,
the boy who, he remembers, would recover fully,
if you overlook the chronic tinge of something
rusted on his breath: now he turns
from the window, he turns
towards the palette with the spot-light

of his brush: he must touch the canvas
only once, he thinks, he must remember
only one thing, to put an end to possibility:
he'll swirl pink and green feathers
through the woman's hair: *Lord,* she sings, *let paradise*
*be clean when I arrive,*
*let it smell of paint-thinner, of formaldehyde.*

## FIRST SNOW: A MEMORY

*During filming, Fred Astaire insisted on so many takes that Ginger Roger's shoes turned pink with blood.*
— American Encyclopedia of Film

I'm watching a movie with my grandfather
who tells me that the snow outside
is the word of God, translated into the intricate
alphabet of the infinite, "like Chinese
characters," he says, so that I turn to listen
to each flake extinguishing itself
against the window, and he turns himself
so completely into his own breathing
that I'm sure, for him, sleep is a hiding place,
a kind of prayer, the snow encasing
his armchair, muffling even the movie.

Which I remember now only as a vague
black-and-white, but which made an impression
so strong that some days, when it snows,
I think of Fred Astaire, knocking loose chips
of plaster from a ceiling so poorly made
it sometimes crumbles on its own. Or I call
each flake a discarded note from music
that evaporates as it plays, as Fred tries
to erase each of Ginger's moves,
to thread them beneath the shadows of his own.

Which is how, from above, we must appear,
trying to thread our particular kind of music
into the landscape, the music of not-having-
anywhere-else-to-go, the tune an exhausted
traveler whistles, not to keep himself awake,
but to bind himself to the emptiness,

making a vacancy inside each note
          where he can curl up and fall asleep.

Years ago, as I was watching the glass
          murder each flake of snow,
my grandfather woke to tell me that, in the end,
          Fred Astaire, defeated from a hundred
takes, collapsed at Ginger's bloody feet.
          I was too young to sense, until now,
what he wanted me to learn: we ruin beauty
          so we can pray for its return.

## THE GREEN BRIDGE

(After *The Chateau des Papes, Avignon* by Paul Signac)

an IV-drip in blues and greens,
          paint applied with a pine needle
or the dry end of the brush:
          here technique is rubbed

to the surface, the modus operandi
          dropping its trenchcoat,
so that the elegant seed-toss
          of a world more loosely connected

than it seems becomes the violence
          of dissection (which conceals
everything equally): a glass-spray
          pointillism, a painting that,

if you could dip your fingers in,
          would break the skin:
call it autopsy-ism, or the biology lab
          where the paint-dipped backs

of insects dazzle through the maze:
          how helpless the landscape
seems: the green bridge, half in collapse,
          dissolving into weeds,

the city, in background, filling
          with dusk, like an upturned hat
with the magician's spell,
          even the sky

the sharpened bird-beak longs
to tap: though it's already been
broken, hasn't it, by the invisible:
jet stream, the barbed wire

of radio waves on a breeze:
here too, in 1900, is the television,
is the pixel, quantum color-
numbered eggs, the information age,

the mind lifting in sequence (let's pretend)
each fleck, so that we can believe
sight is a kind of mending, which engenders
the imagination and makes God

less necessary: last week, at school,
my niece dissected the eye
of a cow: she peeled the lens away
and lowered her blade right down

into the retina, into the rods
and cones: later she said,
jokingly, "we put them back together
so they could see again"

for so long, I'd been thinking
*brick through the greenhouse*
*ceiling, through the solar-housing*
*mind,* that I failed to see that,

flawlessly, the pieces *do* fit back together,
        that here, also, is the world in repair:
mulch-spray, the whole painting
        a candy dish in the humidity

of my color-melting gaze: I failed to see
        that, broken, we already *are*
the scattering, not of ashes,
        but of the visible called back,

endlessly, into the song, we say,
        of matter, which never mouths
the words, but sings: conversation
        through a screen door, a hand

pressed to the speaker-cover's
        mesh: my niece, three nights ago,
laid a piece of tracing paper
        on the cover of a magazine,

and intensely, as if applying make-up
        in a mirror, she sketched
the lines of lips, cheek-bones, hair: and then,
        with care and elegance,

she lifted the face away.

# THE PYRAMIDS OF MALPIGHI

## THE PYRAMIDS OF MALPIGHI

1.
(My Mother's Kidney)

The flaw in it is already set —
something twisted, something clogged —
tiny, impossible to detect,

even for the surgeon who lowers it
into me, carefully, as if he's holding
a nest, as if it could unravel

in his hands, the veins snipped off,
shot straight through, like swords
of light through the magician's box,

so complex and secretive:
who would think they were built
for living things to use?

Mother, some day our bodies
will be discovered
and they will call them ruins.

2.
(News Item)

For seven days, they live in the snow —
a woman and two men —
and then, when the food is gone,
quietly, without ceremony,
they cut into the dead man

with as much precision
as the little knife will give,
because precision, they sense,
is what the dead insist upon.

They cut from the bottom rib
diagonally to the pelvic bone —
to avoid the heart,
to avoid the genitals.

But what can be eaten
after so many days
in the snow? A liver? A spleen?

They gather around the opening,
as if around a fire, as if what's inside
could warm their hands.

Without speaking, but swiftly,
because none of them wants this
to last, they unload him —
sorting, setting aside —

like items from a suitcase:
where will each one go?

3.

In this light, the nephrons are pink,
soft as bread, petal-like, bouqueted
around the flaw, an arrangement

of instances around a now, the molecules
exchanging heat with the doctor's palm,
warming even the latex they move

so casually through. Music's piped in:
eighteenth century strings that vibrate
in the boy's left ear, that vibrate

in the renal artery. The doctors,
in their formal gowns, gather
around the kidney — its cells twirling —

as if it were being served
in a brandy sifter. The photons glitter in the iodine
and the nurse — quite properly,

as if fearing a dollop may drip
onto the tablecloth — stirs
the catheter tip into a dish of lubricant.

4.

If there is an afterlife, it is in the imagination of others.
And resurrection? In the stories that they tell.

5.

Your kidney lived for such a short time
in me — a few hours,
maybe a day. And what did you expect?
Did you think
you could fit inside me, that I would smuggle
you into the skin
of a better life, away from your working-mother
days, a marriage
built on the love of diminishing returns?
Did you think
I was your slick passage out of death?
For years, the doctor
has been holding you above me, as if I were
a tub you were
waiting to fill; for years, you've gazed into me,
preparing to test
my waters with your toe. Tonight, I lift my head
from the table
to see how delicately he holds your kidney,
how tightly you
are curled on his palm, a nest holding something
breakable inside. Mother,
I used to think this room and everything in it
was made of water,
the doctors sloshing in their gowns,
the scalpels
like little fountains, springing from their hands,

the kidney
a whirlpool being sucked into its flaw; I used
to think the boy
on the table really was a tub, that he could be
entered that easily.
Tonight, something freezes, something thaws,
and I can see
the body has no basement, no floor, that it
could never really
hold you. When the doctor lowers you into me,
you drop straight through.

6.

What part of me needs
to feel the little red knife,
the muscles in my hand
working so hard to grip it,

to keep it from falling in?
What part of me needs
to feel that double twitch
of pleasure and disgust

when the flesh gives way?
What part of me needs
to look inside and see
how neatly packed he'd been?

7.

In the instant (1/1,000,000,000th of a second)
after the big bang the universe could fit
inside your living room. In the instant
before that, inside a tea-cup. And so on…

So this is expansion, each moment sliding
into the interior of the next — dark, unbreakable —
gaseous, seemingly amorphous,
steaming with *facts*
                                        (the doctor's hair was brown,
his face was green: "has the patient on the table
had his bowels cleaned?")
                                                            each moment closing
around its flaw, like a fist around a mole,
its *meaning* made infinitely small,
impossible to detect.

But there.
And rigged to expand.

8.

She can't tell if she's rising or falling,
the one who, near dawn, watches the snow
swirl into where their hands
had been, her vision draining,
eventually, into a necklace of icicles
that hangs into the opening, like a mobile
that hangs into a crib, so that she imagines angels
with wings the size of eyebrows,
as if she's traveled this far only to hear
her mother again, playing the piano
in the living room, her fingers
tapping along on the side of the crib,
to see this ring of paper angels swirling
shadows across her forehead again.
If she could rub them from her skin,
she would place them, one by one,
around the opening, as if around a pool,
their legs dangling over the ledge.
She would pray to them. For the dead man,
the fire they dressed him in, and the smoke
that rose, like a wind-blown gown
that reveals the flesh below,
from each piece of him. There is snow, yes,
she is sure of that, but it fails
to stitch the dead man closed. Each flake,
it seems, dips into the opening
and lifts something out of him, like a wheel
of buckets dismantling the water
at the bottom of a stream. Near dawn,
the voices come, distant at first,
like a chorus of women entering
a ravine. She's heard of virgins who sang

even as they were marched to the sacrificial
edge, Mary Queen of Scots, her guillotined
head mouthing, when displayed to the crowd,
the song she must have heard just after death.
Will they come for me? she thinks. What
will it sound like when they arrive?
The snow melts against her forehead,
as if it could slide into her thinking.
Something clicks into place behind her eyes.
*No, that's not how it happened,* it says.
*The fire wouldn't catch,*
*and you ate the dead man cold.*

9.

The anthropologist, my teacher,
cut into the desert to show us the body
he'd discovered
                                        (the heart monitor
signals to the plasma bag)
                                                        and though,
to us, it was little more than a stick-man
drawn in the sand
                                        *(drop drop drop)*
a puppet laid out in his box
in need of a string-master, in need
of a ventriloquist
                                        (beads of blood
stuffed)
                    my teacher tended to him like a mother
preparing her child for school,
using a little brush to sweep clean
the forehead
                    (like sacks of plaques
and globules)
                    polishing the arm-
bones with a cloth
                                        (the leukocytes
orbiting their chromatin)
                                        and digging
out the sand between the rib-bones
and the hips with a little shovel,
something you might use for gardening,
as if he were going to plant something
where the stomach had been. We walked
around the opening
                                        (around tiny radars
that will send them on their pilgrimage)

as if around a pool, our shadows puddled
in the sand, as if birds
                                        (scavenging
through vessel walls)
                                        might land
and drink from them. From above,
there was something vaguely
of a Chinese character
about the arrangement of the bones

(into microscopic tubes)
                                        as if,
at the time of death,
angels
              (that will haul them north)
                                                      had landed
(with the urine)
                              and organized the limbs
into

                                        that when translated
might mean *flock returning*
*to its nest.* Or *full moon over parenthesis*
*undone.* Though when I told this
to my teacher
                              (through the loops
of Henle)
                              he only laughed

(up the cortical arches)<br>
                                        as if life<br>
was comical, and the dead<br>
                                        (until<br>
they open their mouths)<br>
                            the best straight<br>
men. Then he turned back to the shovel,<br>
and to the sand<br>
                            (at the Pyramids)<br>
that, even now, sifts<br>
                            between the bones.<br>
(of Malpighi)<br>
              That will not speak or clot.

10.
Later, so many days later,
they are saved.
A miracle.
News is made.

"Necessity," they say.

"God was with us," they say.

Then they are loaded,
one by one,
onto the waiting plane.

11.
And now the room closes around itself, compressing
            and compressing, greased along its borders
(the universe oiled along its borders) its fault lines exposed,
      walls folding together,
                                    scalpels, clamps, the nurse's pins
melting into a single drop of mercury, all of us —
            doctors, nurses, me — bundled inside the kidney,
our veins slipping inside the sound waves,
            my mother there, our scars sealed together,
an intersection of faces and limbs, cells released
            from their parenthesis, from ownership,
the room made infinitely small, gaseous,
            seemingly amorphous, but already
re-building itself inside a single bead of blood that heals
            and hurts and sings, that at this moment, drops
                                                into me.

12.

A year later, she pours some wine — red, of course — into a coffee cup and slides into the bathtub. Around her neck, she wears a little gold cross that she's taken to sucking into her mouth when she's nervous. She isn't nervous now. It's just, since she's been back, there's a place she always seems to arrive. Something achingly patient that waits for her, like a radio left on in a darkened house. The wine warms her blood until it matches the temperature of the water, and she imagines the strange man entering her house again, a sadly handsome man who exists only as the reflection of himself, leaning over the edge of the tub so she can reach inside and straighten him like a tie. Or no, not handsome this time, but a homely man who turns shy at the sight of her breasts, a boy really, who kneels behind her and steals sips of wine while combing the knots from her hair. "Look at me," he finally says. But when she turns, he spills from himself again, looking out at her through the fabric of the towel on the floor. Yesterday, she went to the movies by herself, a Russian film in which the just-crowned Czar was showered in gold coins, and though she knew this had something to do with power and identity, for her it had everything to do with excess — cells fattening into coins, each emblazoned with an identical face — with how much more body we're given than we'll ever need. Once, in line at the grocery store, she heard a man tell the cashier, "Schizophrenics are the only honest people that I know." And it's true, she thought, she could almost sense herself in the paper bag being stuffed with produce, in the odd collection of coins inside her pocket. She rubs a cloth down the whole length of a thigh, underneath the knee. "Look at me," she says to the water. But really, she wonders, what is it that keeps us from draining into each other, that keeps her consciousness from leaking into the water, the swirling cluster of cells in her brain from pausing, like the map of a storm on a television screen? The empty cup glitters on the ledge of the tub. She leans back, drapes the washcloth over her face, and, at the very edge of a toe, she feels for a drain.

13.

In memory, the boy
beneath the blanket *is*
the excavation, the staked out
property a scar
will build upon, is nothing,

abstract, a piece of wind
lashed through with rain,
his mouth too false
to hold the words
the mask gives back

in a scream of anesthesia.
The face below
is a theory for a face,
a proposal to make
the cells grin,

to make them eyes.
But surely, if the hole
in the blanket can stitch
itself backwards
through the fabric,

if emptiness and matter
can work so beautifully
together, if they can find
their way back
through textiles

and farms to act
as their purest forms —

one a fist of cotton,
            the other an obliterating
wind — then the hole

in the boy must resemble
            this, as in their purest
forms, the room resembles
            its architect, the way
its etchings unraveled

from his hands, the lines
            in the doctor's face
resemble the carvings
            that he's made. My mother
told me once, years ago,

that she had sung me
            into existence, that she sang
for an entire day,
            and her singing became
the snow, and that her song,

falling now, was the snowy part
            of the self, that we are made
of singing and snow,
            and that the singing melts
the snow, and the snow sings back

as it melts to the singing.
            And now the nurse
dissolves into the twitch
            inside her fingers
at the border of a penis,

the swipe she made whistles
          away the catheter,
the pins in her hair become
          their loosening, and the trail
of scorched air

a sound wave leaves
          imitates the music,
the physical reduced
          to its gestures,
until the glittering on the boy

extinguishes the need
          for photons, the need for iodine,
the need for boy, the boy
          set aside to display, more fully,
the opening — so that?

emptiness? the past replaced
          by what it means?
or perhaps, the abstract
          displaced *into* creation
by what it has erased,

the boy's soul burrowing
          through the seen world's
foundation, an invisible
          sheath of amoebae,
countless mouths,

each with a single word inside:
           I   I   I   I
   I   I   I   I
          But no, even then,
there's no stopping it,

the covering up — the fabric
          weaves together to build
an opening, the room
          breaks into walls, the boy's
cells arrange his face,

the kidney drawn into
          the orbit of its flaw.
And the music, insistent,
          as if it could seal
these openings, these pores …

# THE LAST ICEHOUSE IN MINNESOTA

## SECRETARIAL SCHOOL GRADUATION DANCE, 1968

It's strange to think of ourselves
as sperm and egg, our DNA

zipping together, joined along a seam,
23 chromosomes gripping

the other 23 like the dance partners
on the night my parents met.

If there is music in chromosomes
it is built by starlight,

but all the school could afford was a DJ,
a few bowls of punch, and trays layered

with crackers, cheese and squares of ham.
They could not afford to have moonlight

drawn through the windows
by the lacquer on the slick gym floor.

Even my mother's dress
had been worn by her sister

to the same dance the year before.
Still, I would like to have been there.

I would like to have been
the extra tooth in my father's grin,

or the piece of candy my mother
offered him from her purse.

If we lived within our parents'
bodies, traveling from port

to tiny port in their veins,
light funneling in

through their mouths, I think
it must have been the sturdiest form

of heaven, sealed in the adjoining rooms
of our own history.

But who could live as a fraction?
My father couldn't.

I like to think I helped him
overcome his shyness that night,

that I drew the sweat back
into his palms, loosened his tie

so his words could break free.
Or maybe I was just outside

them both, a single beat in the music,
the one that played when she bent —

just long enough to get
a look at his shoes —

and saw him shift his grip
from her shoulder

to her waist, slowly, in a distracted way,
as if by accident.

# ROMANCE

*For My Grandfather*

The wind that returned you from the war,
that sent the bullet aimed for the pocket
in your shirt skidding into the dirt,

the wind that turned your face to the sky,
filling your lungs with sunlight,
and carried away the voice that said,

*boy, you've lived your last cold winter*
*in Iowa,* is the same wind that trailed
behind you as you hauled halves of beef

from refrigerated box-cars to a cooler,
shifting the slabs from shoulder to shoulder,
in a meat packing plant in Des Moines

on the day you and my grandmother met.
In the inspection room, the fans cooled
the meat, numbing her fingers and loosening

the strings of her apron when she bent
to remove a scrap of fat from her shoe.
You worked there thirty-five years,

and if you were here now you'd say
*to hell with that plant*, you'd take it apart
bolt by bolt, stack the steel girders

and i-beams back onto steamboats
that delivered them from the foundries
of Pittsburgh, you'd tow the box-cars

back to the slaughterhouse, peel up
the tracks behind them. Grandfather,
do you think the war made you tough?

I'll show you. I rebuild that plant. I rebuild
the fans, the hooks, the drip pans below
that gather the blood. I re-pour the concrete

floor, stoke the coals that move
the cars. I revive the cattle, the grass
that fed them, all the months from the war

to then, my grandmother, her bending.
I sew her an apron, not for the sake
of romance, but for the loosening strings.

And when I rebuild your own young body
from muscled sunlight, sweat, and calluses,
I will send it on its way to re-tie them.

## SHINGLES

Today, my grandfather's muscles are an answer
to the blizzard that battered and tore the shingles
from his roof, an answer to the wind that tries
and tries to lift his shadow from the wood.

He pounds each new shingle into place,
as if to say, *there, you won't be doing that again.*
His hammering startles birds from the ledge,
but can't drown out his off-key singing:

*the work, the working, just the working life ...*

His voice travels through the eaves, onto the splash-
block, into the lawn and below the grass
where it is 1923, and a late-April storm keeps
his father from the fields, sending him from room

to room, whistling and flipping his pocket-
watch open and closed, his boredom warming
into lust, on the day his eleventh child, my grandfather,
is conceived. On the sofa, my great-grandmother

shuffles the cards for a game of Crazy Eight,
her hands deep in habit, her mouth hot from scolding
the children. By now, even her thoughts
are small children, scurrying, bold and un-chaperoned,

through her mind, locking themselves into tiny rooms
and giggling. When he comes to her,
when he sends the boys out to shovel the long drive
and leads her to the bed, unbuckling the tops

of his overalls on the way, she thinks of herself

as the snow, swooning and drifting against the side
of the house. The storm mounts and mounts
inside her, the snow fusing into my grandfather's

bones, the wind slipping between each flake
to become his singing. Now, that snow melts
into the sweat at the back of his neck,
the saliva building and receding in his mouth.

If he thinks of his mother at all, if he hears her
in the soft cry each bent and rusted nail makes
when he yanks it from the wood, it doesn't interfere
with his work. He will strike the last nail

long past exhaustion, his shoulders tight
from swinging the hammer, his throat closing
around its thirst, even as he carries his song
into the lawn, his voice drifting and swooning—

*out with the old, and in with the new*
*lost my hat and replaced it with a shoe …*

The weathered shingles lie scattered near
the edge of the house, some of them
like tiny shut doors to the past, others
flipped open and open by the wind.

The last thing she said to him was, "Climb up
to the roof and see if you can get rid
of that awful sun." Years from now, when
nearly every day from his childhood

has fallen to the floor of his memory
and shattered, he will think of the storm
his mother told him of, he will think it is best
to die, not in your sleep, but in a wind

so fierce it swoops you in and drags you
back to the moment when the odds
against your birth crumbled, the first cry,
not yours, but your mother's, her legs

raised in a rehearsal of labor. How else
would you know that even the worst
of your history was a series of conquests?
How else would you know that you had won?

# IN CELEBRATION OF MY FATHER'S 35TH YEAR AT THE COCA-COLA COMPANY

All day he drives the highways
of Minnesota, past the obstacle-course
of construction between Waseca
and Madison Lake, the trees he's seen
a thousand times, both empty and full,
near the Iowa border, wind and velocity
bending the van's antenna,
blurring the letters of the company logo
on the huge side door. He stops
at every *Red Owl* and *Super-Value*
on the way to calculate the week's sales,
arrange the displays, as on the drive
back — a sunset shelved on the horizon,
going flat as his can of soda on the dash —
he might arrange his inventory of shaken
hands, calculate the little loss
for little pay of each working day,
the doubled pull of a road, forward
and home, where he will toss
his checkbook and then his wallet
on the counter, and walk
to the bathroom to shower before dinner.
In the morning, he will not shower
again, only splash sleep and the night's
small dreams from his face, his hands
cupped into a tiny boat, the way
he takes his communion on Sundays.
Some mornings, he stays bent
over the sink, pumping his arms
up and down, slow and mechanical,
as if he could stay there the rest
of the day, loading and unloading the water.

## ADOLESCENCE

If we are drawn to things it's by
                    the absence we sense inside of them:
my father's clothes, for instance,
                    not his scent, faint from the washings,
but persistent, that leads me to his
                    closet, but their lack of resistance, how easily
they display the form inside them,
                    the way, at adolescence, the body displays —
with blemishes, strange sproutings
                    of hair, oils that light the face — the confusion that,
since birth, has grown inside it,
                    like grass, untended, that the mind bends to, that
the mind tears off in bits. I walk,
                    split at the waist by my father's work-shirt,
to the kitchen, where I find the pot,
                    emptied of its coffee, though a bit of steam
still nests inside the glass — the way
                    thought nests, for an instant, inside the mind,
then goes — a plate, lit with crumbs,
                    at the bottom of the sink, the crumbs trying
to congeal into a fingertip when I
                    touch at them, trying to rent out a little space
in the skin, which is how, at birth,
                    light must've felt, trying to press its way into
the body, trying to pull the body
                    closed behind it. At adolescence, boys are taught
that it's not OK to kiss your father
                    on the lips, to reach out through the eyes and
embrace your father's form when
                    he rises from the tub, they are taught a covert
affection, a code made of little pun-
                    ches, nicknames like "sport" and "chief" and "ace,"
words that don't linger too long

on the tongue, the benign twins of "honey" and
"sweetheart" and "darling," they
are taught resistance and even to distrust
the balder forms of love, which is
how jealousy is born, and indifference.
My father took me once, on his route,
to help arrange the displays, coke bottles balanced
on top of each other, the two of us
working, one from each end, stacking the cases
between us. Later, at the final stop
of the day, I turned to him and said, "I'll wait here
in the truck." What lesson was I
trying, with a voice more bored than I was,
to give back to him? And what part
of me still wishes he would've whipped my ass
for that? Father, what is a fist but
a way to make an ending, a way to crank the zero
closed? My chief, my ace, years
ago, I stole one of your shirts to remind myself
of how easily we fit inside each
other, and this morning, when I unbuckle
my belt, I am tucking myself
into your absence. Do you see how simple
it is? Even then, even now:

two hands orbiting a waist.

## FORGIVENESS

At lunch, your friend tells you he's having trouble with his lover and you say, "I'm sorry," which doesn't seem to help much, because he's really swimming in it now, so drenched with tears you half-expect the waiter to stop by and sponge him off. So you swipe a few napkins from their little tin house, lean across the table and say, "I'm really, really sorry," like you're asking for his forgiveness. Which, after all, maybe you are, because the scroll of your own sins, when it comes to love, could stretch from here to the men's room and back, and part of you wants to unroll it right now, and start listing them off, like they do at hangings. But seeing your friend wrecked like this makes the other part of you feel lousy and really wish for his forgiveness, or if not his, then the waiter's, or well, at this point, anyone's would do. Because that's the way the world should work, you think, we should forgive each other all the time, handshakes cut loose in favor of gestures of forgiveness, a palm placed upon the forehead of everyone you meet, their palm on your forehead, leaning there against each other, a few absolving words, little post-it notes — *don't be so hard on yourself* — stuck to your computer at work, even just a quick sign-of-the-cross from your boss on his way to the john. So that you could forgive him when he comes back again, for surely he'd have sinned in those few minutes, and you would have too, one of those small malices — a shameful, held-in fart, slamming your desk drawer because the work never stops — the misdemeanors we all commit, because, eventually, even the good must sin, if for nothing else, then for the joy forgiveness brings. And why not give that to each other all the time? Though maybe we already do this, because what else would you call them, except gestures of forgiveness, that upward swipe that says it's OK your fly is down, a hand extending towards a mislaid hair, or something subtler than that, the quick glance in the hallway that says "here we both are, and that's OK," the two minds processing and judging, judging and releasing, both knowing so much about the shortcomings of the other, yet arranging an oblivious face, like the waiter who ignores the napkins, crumpled with tears and snot, your friend has left piled on his plate.

## CHIMES

How easily, this morning, the rain enters the snow, drilling finger-holds, as if destruction could make the world grippable.

> Watching the spring rain
> I ask: how deep into earth
> does our vision go?

I stand before my parents' bay window, listening to the wind-chime that hangs like an audacious earring on the porch, as if the house were trying to attract a mate. Behind me, I can hear my mother in the kitchen, listening to Pavarotti, while she sweeps the floor, while she bakes. When I visit, I like to listen to her sing, I like to listen to the music enter her and sing back out through her throat.

> No need for a spoon.
> The music will stir itself
> into the batter.

How does she sing so flawlessly in a language she does not know? Where is the seam inside me where the two voices meet? Lately, she gets confused about things. Wind chimes, for instance.

> She thinks they measure
> temperature, she thinks, sometimes,
> that they're shivering.

On one wall, she's hung the picture of a flooded city-street, the surface of the water strung between the second-story windows of the row houses, circa 1950, as if the beautiful housewives of Cedar Rapids could grip the flood along the edges and snap the wrinkles free. My mother told me once,

"They lost everything.
Water that deep even strips
houses of their paint."

She touched her fingers to the photo, as if she could dip them in and start emptying the stream: lawn furniture and pets, toys, morning papers swept from the islands of their welcome mats, the collective unconscious of a small-town block. But no, it's more than that: it's history. In Napoleon's biography, his emissaries mounted the fastest horses in all of France to meet his carriage with correspondence, notes, and maps he discarded — scraps of paper scattered like lamps to light the road to his defeat.

Some ripped by weather,
some found, some, crumpled, that held
the lines of his palm.

"Don't wash," he wrote back
one winter to Josephine.
"I'm coming home."

When I tell her this, my mother stirs a question mark into the chocolate sauce I smell burning on the stove. When she gets confused about things, thinking, for instance, that wind-chimes signal the passage of time, she twists her hair into knots.

She picks at the lines
of my palm. She lifts them out,
pins her hair with them.

On bad days, she forgets my name, what season it is, where things go. Something inside her is drawing itself across the surface of everything she knows, and this morning, watching the rain fall into the snow —

The snow opening
now, like the mouths of fish,
to take each drop in —

I think of this as a kind of clarity. A thought drops; the mind, refigured, cinches closed. Outside, a boy is walking home, slipping easily between the rain and the snow, a few drops ending on his tongue.

Mother, even now,
there is the sound of wind-chimes
nearby, and of hooves.

## MANHOLE COVERS AND LAKES

My love for manhole covers is also a love of lakes, and together they are a love for the abstract, a belief that the seen world has depths beyond those we perceive. The mathematics of sewers and waves, in other words, is all about negative numbers. The problem with negative numbers, of course, is that they imply that the future and past travel at an identical velocity. Which is why I don't love negative numbers. I do love mathematics, though, the consistency of waves hinting that the fish below swim along predetermined tracks. I've even called this beauty, though it's really little more than a love for psychology, present shaped by past, and which reminds me that my love for manhole covers is also a love of sex and secrecy (those little drilled finger-holes, clotted with darkness). My love of lakes is also a love for the fingerprints of waves, which is really a love for the shapelessness of identity, and for Narcissus who, exhausted, scooped his reflection from the water and washed his two faces with each other. There isn't much to do with a love for manhole covers and lakes. At best, it reminds me of other silly things, like how, as a boy, when my mother wasn't looking, I stole the cap from a gallon of milk and hid it beneath my tongue. And how, after searching the kitchen, she leaned over to inspect my mouth, and I felt the future seal together inside me, as it only can when what happens is so precisely what we hadn't known we'd planned.

# THE LAST ICEHOUSE IN MINNESOTA

*— State law requires all ice-fishing houses to be removed from lakes by midnight on March 15th.*

1.

It takes a certain devotion
to tend the last house
on the lake, like a chapel left
behind when the faithless town
has moved away, the smoke
from the chimney
a signal that the lake's
still here: *all's well, all's*
*well.* Though deep
in its enormous basement
the carp tire of perfecting
their hungry art,
erasing and erasing
the signatures of leaches
and worms, the lake
drawing, always, two more
into the water behind them.
And the man who walks
the ceiling, tending the well,
using a spoon to scrape
away the curls of ice,
grows weary of lighting
and re-lighting
the little wood stove.

2.

Some mornings,
when I see him set
out, exhausted
but un-wavered
by the fracturing ice,
his head bobbing back
and forth in the boat
of its own fatigue,
I'm sure I'm looking
at a ghost. What else
to call him, this man
who swerves so surely
above his own deep
history, like a captain
crossing the deck
of some long-ago ark
on his way to inspect
the diminishing loot
in the hatches below,
the matches dry
in his boots,
dry in his boots …

# INSIDE THE DIALYSIS MACHINE

## INSIDE THE DIALYSIS MACHINE

1.
Matter is all we have, and all we have
to lose

is inside the dialysis machine,
excess water drained,

phosphorous and sodium like crumbs
brushed from a sleeve,

as if separation were the real art,
the blood destroyed and rebuilding itself

like notes of a song at the moment of inspiration,
not created, but suddenly remembered

when all other noise inside the composer's brain
has been siphoned away:

inside the dialysis machine, all symmetry
is broken symmetry, the illusion

of the fixed interior revealed like a cloth
swiped from the top of a birdcage,

a hand reaching through the little metal door
altering the motion inside

so that when the blood collides
with the dialystate, the lethal cells are divided

from the clean, *almost* systematically,
as if there is a *decision*, the mind of the cell

unlocked, that single orbiting thought
that, if we are quiet enough,

pours through every opening, the frequency
of the electron made audible, a finger

dipped in water and circling the rim
of a glass: today, in the salt mines of Ohio

scientists are watching vats of water
through computer screens,

trying to observe, for the first time,
proton decay, a bit of light that will demonstrate

how all matter dissolves, eventually, into energy:
inside the dialysis room, even our bodies

are reduced to their frequencies, plugged in,
as if their diminishment was powering

the machines, as if the purpose of motion
was to make matter clean,

stirring the batter of us until the lumps
scatter and dissolve, while

on the other side of the room, a nurse,
absentmindedly, divides the pills —

one blue, one red, one green —

into the pyramid of paper cups
she's balanced on a tray.

2.

If you believe the spirit can be siphoned
away, you must also believe

in its return: at fifteen, for instance,
I spent a year unraveling

and being sewn back together,
one long thread of me

being fed into the dialysis machine,
like a reel of film through a projector,

as if I could lay myself down,
frame by frame, into the plastic tube

and make my life seen: ice chips,
blankets and saline heated

to 98 degrees, a life reduced
to its necessities, not just for me,

but for all of us in the dialysis
room, leaving ourselves

at the velocity of trains, rattling
through our chills and our coughing fits:

Charlie, with his ritual of phrase, "time
to get the oil changed:"

Wendy outtalking any audience —
a husband dead, a toy poodle yipping

towards the grave — until her own eyes
finally closed, and she curled up

inside the little padded basket
of her brain: and Abbie, the only girl

my age, sixteen and a prisoner
of headphones, humming the Beatles,

though I kept hearing:
*we all live*

*in a dialysis machine, dialysis*
*machine, dialysis machine:*

she loved Jackson Pollack, too:
"he makes the paint so alive,"

she said, "you can almost hear it sing:"
and why not believe, at sixteen, that a man

could paint himself free of his body,
not just symbolically,

but weaving above the canvas,
like a cut boxer across the ring:

why not believe, at fifteen, that a man
could be stripped to his veins,

that it was possible to live wholly inside
the dialysis machine, my imperfections —

zits, bad grades — being scrubbed
away — like night drained of its bats —

while I emptied towards sleep,
my body deflating, buoyant

as a tablecloth tossed
across the waves, my body

thin as a handkerchief
pulled from a sleeve.

3. Pollock At Work

What does it mean: the false
pattern everywhere, the wind-

shifted weather map his cigarette
leaves in the air, paint-splattered

boots, an elaborate cage of laces
strapping down the leather tongue:

is this the end of speech, of the insistence
of the brush: inside the dialysis room,

a party's being made, streamers hung,
our bodies improvising from the sheet music

of our DNA, being drawn through machines,
like breath through an instrument,

something terribly nimble catching
all the fingerings

so the destructive cells are dropped away:
inside the machine, the past is reduced

to its energy, memories colliding,
scattered into fractured imagery,

Pollock at work, moving instinctively
above the canvas, like hands

across a Ouija board, trying to paint
the underneath, laying down the ungatherable

thread for the eye to retrieve, the paint
unraveling, it seems, from his sleeve:

inside the dialysis room, we can't stop
being translated back into ourselves,

words lifted from the telegraph tape
back onto our tongues, excess letters gone,

so *inspiration* becomes *ration*
*surface* becomes *face*

and the wind blows back the hood
of the horizon: if we wake refreshed,

it's because our subconscious
has been drained, Abbie and I bending

beneath the bridge of our sleep,
waist-deep in the stream of us

*these are the strong, troubled,*
*murderous thinkings of the masculine sea*

clearing out the twigs and fallen leaves
*these the gentle thoughts of the feminine air*

the waves brushing starlight through
our pubic hair: what does it mean

to swerve away from form,
an icicle softening on the tip

of a brush — *drip, drip, drip* —
everything melting now, paint spilled

across the surface of the lake:
is it beauty we are passing through —

the motions of the body
slurred across the canvas —

before we are launched back
into ourselves, refigured,

accidental and clean:
what does it mean to refuse beauty —

our flaws seeping in again
when our blood touches form —

to refuse the permission of the saints:
if there is no opposite to god

who bleached this canvas white
for him to paint.

Note: The parenthetical lines are taken from *Moby Dick*.

4.

When the little brick house
I think of as the past

collapses and rebuilds itself
as a garden wall, a gazebo now,

now a shed, I think that even time
must be filtered through the dialysis machine,

each moment happening until it comes back clean,
so that when I circle back to that room

it's to the light inside it, to its mood,
all of us reduced to our particles

so that the mind can rebuild us
as I please: lines of motion and paint,

or as the passengers on a train,
a boy and a girl with their seats tilted back,

faces angled towards each other,
their fingers inching towards each other

as their lives drain in opposite directions:
all night, they whisper each other

through the dark, speaking of the future,
which is a locked museum to them,

the security guard's flashlight swiping
a path across the paint, like the headlight

of a train: they laugh; they tuck their jackets
beneath their chins, like blankets,

because it's getting cold, and the wheels below
are eating the moonlight off the tracks.

5.

Something, somewhere was taking it all down —
clipping the phone lines,

a ladder with its rungs blown free,
all the vacant nests

restored to twigs — until even the snow
was a wind-shattered ghost,

or the interior of bread
imprinting its absence

against the false mouths of windows:
we looked out, entranced —

by which I mean the consciousness
sings a little around the eyes —

as if the wind could sway
the lines inside the dialysis room,

where our ticketed cells were being
oared into the flume,

the self foaming into a not-yet-
entirely-new solution,

the self, as always, trying to oar its way
out of the body,

the nurse delivering pills on schedule,
our names printed on the sides

of the cups: Abbie reached over,
once, to work a kink out of my tube —

her hand crossing and re-crossing
the tight rope between me

and the machine — and left a fingerprint
smeared into my blood:

something, somewhere was taking it
all down: temperature, fluid intake,

hemoglobin and creatinine, leukocytes,
erythrocytes, a census of the blood,

numbers the machine worked to calibrate:
the drowned cells, the fat cells dragging

in the blood, cells that rotated backwards,
cells with a hole burned through,

cells that kept a scream in them,
that kept time in them, the blind

and mirroring cells, cells that drained
into each other, the vanishing

cells (no less real for that), goblet
and chalice cells, the branded,

clenched and potted cells, cells
that needed watering, the watery

cells the seen world dived through
in the brain, cells that inflated,

that translated, cells that buttoned down
a face, the robed cells of memory:

outside, men cleared the parking lot
of snow, each shovel-full —

a brief structure of its own —
torn open in the air, the touched moment

swirling up from the surface, swirling up
into a mind: we were homesick inside

the dialysis machine
for the stick-figure versions of ourselves:

we wanted to be form again: but we kept passing
through the typewriter ribbon

of our own histories — something, somewhere
was taking it all down —

the sleeping present rising to take
the removable part of each

moment in: and things were coming
apart inside, seams unraveling

from the fabric of the chairs,
the faithful interior being led astray

until I thought I could heal myself
in everything: trinity of pills, muscle

of the blood-pressure cuff, the flung snow,
my reflection wrapped around an IV pole:

something, somewhere was taking it all down,
casting us into all those doubled

tubes that hung in the air, like pairs of lips,
between Abbie and me,

as if we were being exchanged for each other
(here is your reflection, a playbook for your gesturing)

or staining the chemical rinse of each other's
imagining, Abbie with a thermometer

in her mouth, her speech, the wind-swept
debris of the mind, defrosting

the mercury, as if ideas,
like vague erections at adolescence,

could be measured only by the pleasure
of their leaving: "When we die,"

she said, "I think we become a part
of time, broken and borderless, spiraling

out in all directions, like a listening:"
I am giving her these words now

because only absence is permanent —
something, somewhere was taking it all

down — and when I step back into that room —
or what could be gleaned — I hear

the voices — from inside the dialysis machine —
plural at first, linked, and must

divide them into throats: I hear the sound
of machines beneath the speech,

and then I just hear speech.

## ABOUT THE AUTHOR

Steven Gehrke is the winner of the 2002 Philip Levine Prize for Poetry for his manuscript, *The Pyramids of Malpighi,* selected by Philip Levine. He received a B.S. in English from Minnesota State University, Mankato and an M.F.A. from the University of Texas, where he was a James Michener Fellow. At publication time, he was a Ph.D. candidate at the University of Missouri. His poems have been anthologized in *American Poetry: The Next Generation* (Carnegie Mellon Press), and have appeared in *Indiana Review, Gulf Coast, Many Mountains Moving, Mississippi Review,* and *The Georgia Review.* His first book of poems, *The Resurrection Machine,* was selected by Miller Williams as winner of the John Ciardi Prize for Poetry, and published by BkMk Press in 2000.